START YOUR ENGINES!



# DRAGSTERS

By Martha London

Kaleidoscope
Minneapolis, MN

**The Quest for Discovery Never Ends**

*This edition first published in 2020 by Kaleidoscope Publishing, Inc.*



*For information regarding permission, write to
Kaleidoscope Publishing, Inc.
6012 Blue Circle Drive
Minnetonka, MN 55343*

*Library of Congress Control Number
2019940176*

*ISBN
978-1-64519-054-7 (library bound)
978-1-64494-212-3 (paperback)
978-1-64519-155-1 (ebook)*



*Printed in the United States of America.*

**Bigfoot lurks within one of the images in this book. It's up to you to find him!**

# TABLE OF CONTENTS

## CHAPTER 1

# Built for Speed

Tia is strapped into the driver's seat with a harness. She wears a helmet. Her racing suit zips up to her neck. She knows the Funny Car's engine is roaring. But she can't hear it. She's focused on the track ahead. Her Funny Car is as powerful as a Top Fuel dragster. But the car's body is shorter. It looks like a bigger version of a regular car. Its rear tires are much bigger than regular car tires.

*Funny cars are similar to regular cars, but they are low to the ground and have huge rear tires.*

The **chassis** is covered by an outer shell. Metal bars surround Tia. They form a roll cage. The bars will protect her if the car loses control and flips.

Another Funny Car sits next to Tia. That's her competition. Drag races are usually between just two cars. Racers want to see which car can **accelerate** fastest. Tia takes a deep breath. The race begins. Tia takes off!

Tia is pressed against her seat. The car accelerates quickly. She holds on to the steering handles. She doesn't need to do much turning. The black asphalt stretches out in a straight line.

Everything outside is a blur. Computer timers switch gears for Tia. The car accelerates too fast for her to do it herself. She nears the finish line. As she crosses it, a flag waves. But she can't see it. She's still going more than 300 miles per hour (483 km/h).

The track goes on past the finish line. She has plenty of room to slow down. Even with brakes, it takes a long time to stop.

**FUN FACT**

**Top Fuel dragsters accelerate from 0 to 100 miles per hour (160 km/h) in less than 0.8 seconds.**

*Drag racers go so fast that a force equal to five times their body weight pushes back on them.*

She pushes the button for the parachute. It opens behind her car. The parachute fills with air. This creates **drag**. The drag slows the car down quickly. Tia braces against the force. She's glad to have the harness.

Her car slows to a stop. The car next to her does, too. Tia's team rushes over to her. They congratulate her on a great win. She made it to the finish line in 3.8 seconds.

**FUN FACT**

Dragster parachutes must be carefully packed and secured to the car before each race.

Dragsters have parachutes to help drivers slow down at the end of a race.

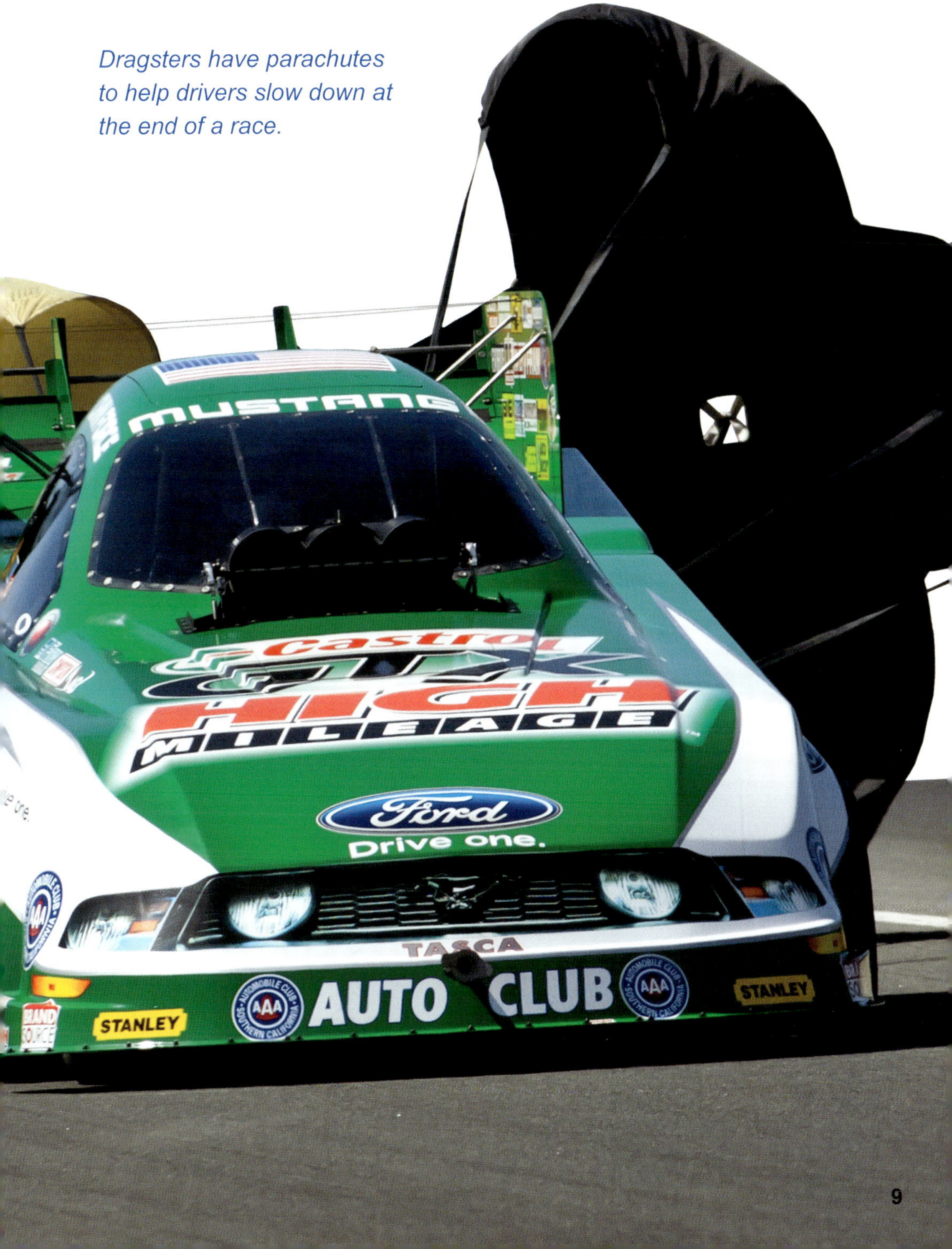

CHAPTER 2

# Beat the Clock

In the 1930s, people worked on **hot rods**. They raced in dry lake beds. They wanted to see how fast they could go. But they had a new goal in 1949. They wanted to see how fast they could accelerate. They needed more space. Utah was the place to go.

People spread the word. The event would be called Speed Week. Racers would compete to see who could accelerate fastest. Hot rods gathered at the Bonneville Salt Flats. A wide stretch of flat ground lay in front of them.

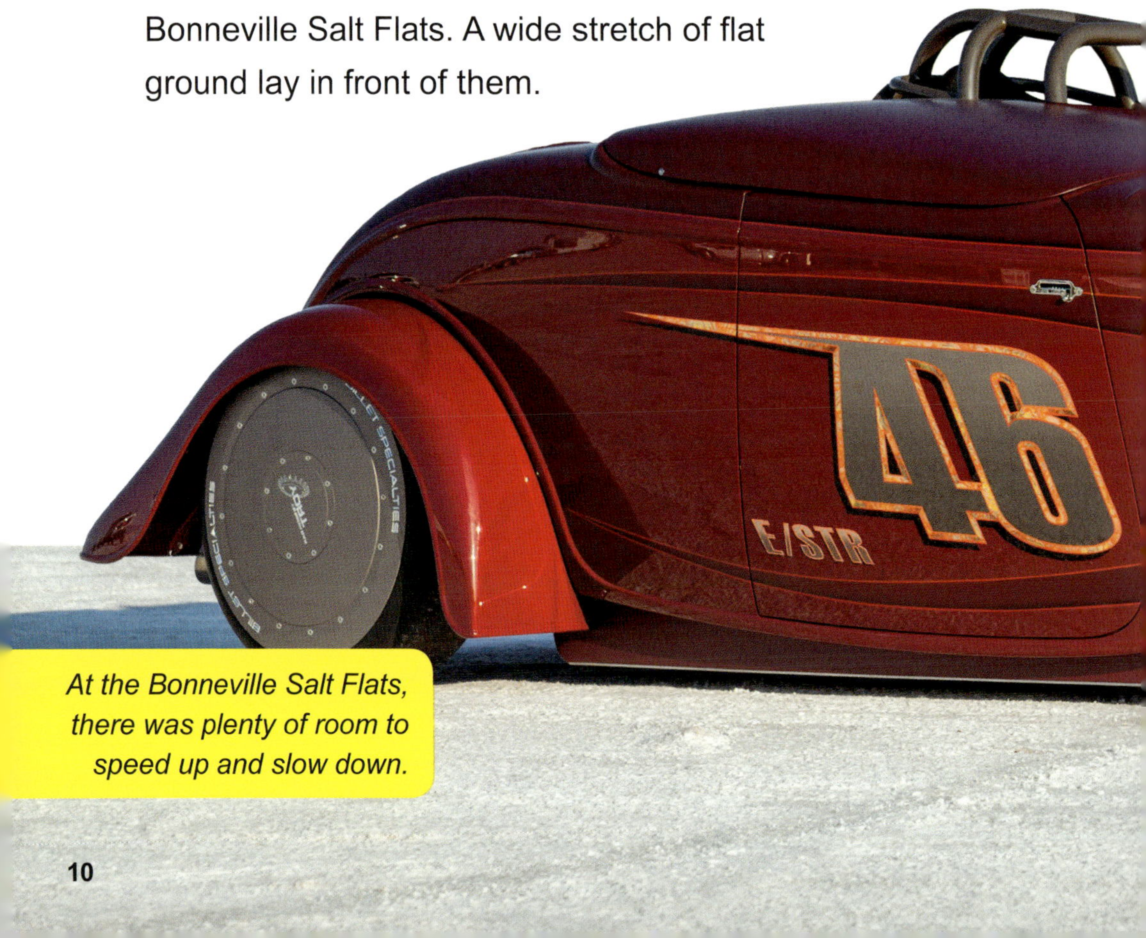


*At the Bonneville Salt Flats, there was plenty of room to speed up and slow down.*

A racer pushed his hot rod to the starting line. The sound of rumbling engines filled the air. He pulled goggles over his eyes. Almost as soon as the race started, it was over. The car had zoomed to over 100 miles per hour (160 km/h) in 21 seconds.

*Early dragsters were hot rods, but over time, dragsters were heavily modified and now have completely different engines and appearances.*

**FUN FACT**

**The National Hot Rod Association (NHRA) was formed in 1951. It created safety guidelines.**

## DIVERSITY IN DRAGSTERS

**Most drag racers are white men. But people of color and women are starting to become stars. In 2012, Antron Brown became the first African American racer to win a major title. Courtney Force is another drag racer. In 2017, she won her one hundredth race. She was the first woman to do so.**

Over time, dragsters and hot rods divided. Hot rods had normal engines. They used gasoline. Dragsters had supercharged engines. They used special fuel. Dragsters also had **modified** chassis. This made them faster than hot rods.

Drag racing became popular. Race tracks were built. Crowds didn't have to watch from the ground. People sat in bleachers. They loved watching the cars burn rubber.

Don Garlits was an early drag racer. Traditionally, engines were in the front of the car. But that was more dangerous. In 1970, something went wrong. Part of the engine exploded. This caused Garlits to lose part of his foot. He helped design a new style of dragster. The engine was behind the driver.

Some people laughed at Garlits. They thought his dragster wouldn't work. But it won race after race. And it was much safer.

In 1992, history was made again. Kenny Bernstein got in his dragster. He launched from the starting line. A sign showed his time and speed. He was the first driver to break 300 miles per hour (483 km/h).

| DRAGSTER TYPE | TOP FUEL DRAGSTER | FUNNY CAR | PRO STOCK CHEVY CAMARO |
|---|---|---|---|
| WEIGHT | 2,320 pounds (1,050 kg) | 2,575 pounds (1,168 kg) | 2,350 pounds (1,065 kg) |
| TOP SPEED | 330 miles per hour (530 km/h) | 330 miles per hour (530 km/h) | 213 miles per hour (342 km/hr) |
| BASE PRICE | $275,000 | $300,000 | $250,000 |
| FEATURES/ SPECIAL FEATURES | • Rear engine<br>• Rear wing<br>• Multistage clutch activated by timers | • Carbon fiber body<br>• Extra-large rear tires<br>• Multistage clutch activated by timers | • Custom chassis for aerodynamics<br>• Up to 1300 horsepower<br>• Closely resembles factory car |

DRAGSTERS

# SIDE BY SIDE

## Top Fuel Dragster

## Funny Car

## Pro Stock Chevy Camaro

CHAPTER 3

# Three, Two, One

Leah Pritchett stands with her team. Pritchett is a Top Fuel racer. Top Fuel cars got their name from the type of fuel they use. **Nitromethane** burns fast and hot. It gives the car a lot of power.

Pritchett's team still needs to build the engine. Dragsters are complicated machines. The race lasts only 4 seconds. In that time, **spark plugs** melt. Tires can blow out.

Mechanics rebuild dragster engines after every race and make sure everything is working safely.

Cracks appear in the chassis. Dragsters are rebuilt after every race.

Pritchett helps her team unload the equipment. Crowds will start to gather soon. The team needs to focus. Mechanics and crew assistants get to work. Everyone looks over the equipment. Pritchett is the driver. She looks over her dragster, too.

Top Fuel cars are long and narrow. This one is red and black. The front tires are small. But the rear tires are huge. A rear wing rises above the back of the car. It forces air down onto the car. This presses the car down. The tires keep their grip on the track.

*Top Fuel dragsters have huge rear wings to move air down onto the car.*

The mechanics check tire pressure. Their tools clank. Next, the mechanics assemble the engine. They tighten screws. Nothing can be out of place. The car is carefully inspected. If a single piece doesn't work correctly, the dragster could explode.

The engine is secured. Now it's time for the fuel. Pritchett pours the nitromethane into the fuel tank. The engine will drink more than 22 gallons (83 L) today.

**FUN FACT**

Top Fuel dragsters cover the length of four football fields in less than five seconds.

# ZOOM IN ON A TOP FUEL DRAGSTER

Crew members screw the cover over the fuel tank. Pritchett puts on her suit. It is made of a special material. The fabric protects Pritchett from fire if there is an accident. She pulls the sleeves over her arms. She zips up the suit. She's almost ready.

The crew moves the car toward the starting line. Pritchett puts on her helmet. It's stuffy, but it keeps her safe. She climbs into the driver's seat. The crew chief pulls the top down. He shuts her into the dragster. Pritchett is ready to race.

*Top Fuel racer Leah Pritchett makes sure to wear her suit and helmet to protect herself during the race.*

CHAPTER 4

# A Quarter Mile to Glory

AJ is a Pro Stock racer. Pro Stock cars are based on cars that come from the factory. They are like regular cars. But they are much more powerful.

Pro Stock racers don't go as fast as Top Fuel racers. But AJ will go faster than 200 miles per hour (320 km/h). AJ trusts his team. He has worked with them for years.

*Pro Stock cars look similar to everyday cars, but they have many modifications to make them more powerful.*

*Cars have to meet exact measurements in order to qualify for the Pro Stock class.*

AJ drives up to the starting line. He looks over at the other driver. He nods. The sky is cloudy. That's good for driving. There's no glare on the strip.

The engine hums. AJ presses his foot on the pedal. His car leaps forward. He doesn't look at the car next to him.

**FUN FACT**

A Pro Stock car engine is eight times more powerful than the average car's engine.

He has to focus on the track. He needs to keep his car in a straight line.

Both cars fly down the racing strip. In less than seven seconds, the race is done. Their parachutes work perfectly. AJ didn't win this one. But the **adrenaline** of racing is what he enjoys.

Later on, AJ sits in the stands. The Funny Car races are beginning. Two Funny Cars line up at the starting line. The two cars do a **burnout** on the track. Smoke rises from the cars' tires. The burnout gives the tires better grip for the race. People chat as the cars reverse to the starting line. Crew members wave the racers to the right position.

The crowd goes silent. The sound of the engines is deafening. Lights count down: three, two, one. Flames fly out from the exhaust pipes. Heads whip to follow the fast cars. AJ cheers when they cross the finish line.

## TOP FUEL DRAGSTER

# HOW BIG IS A TOP FUEL DRAGSTER?

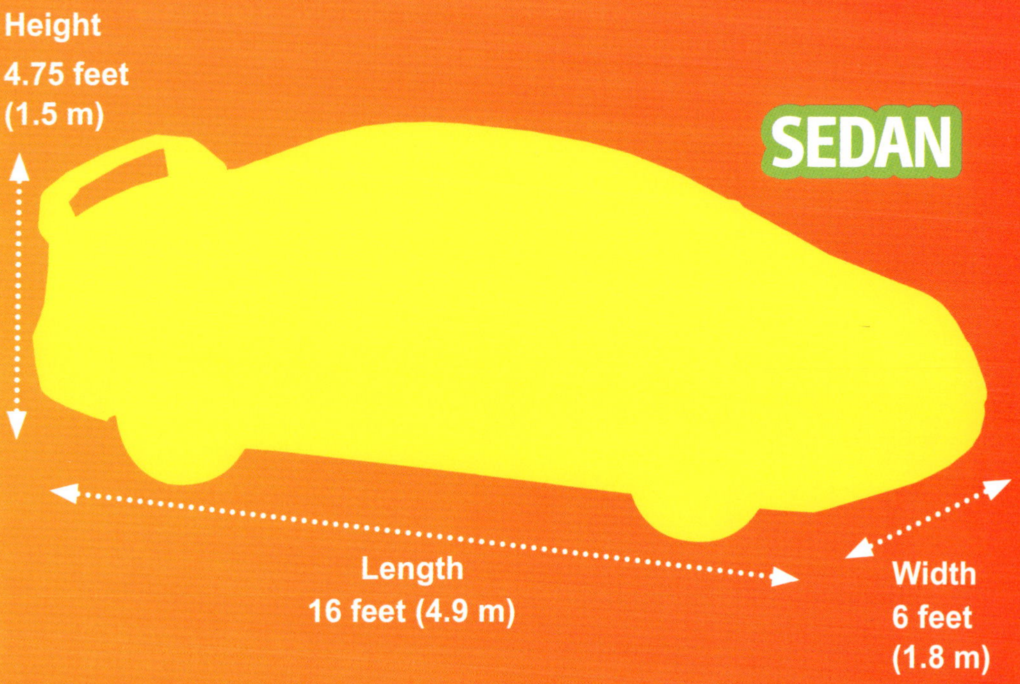


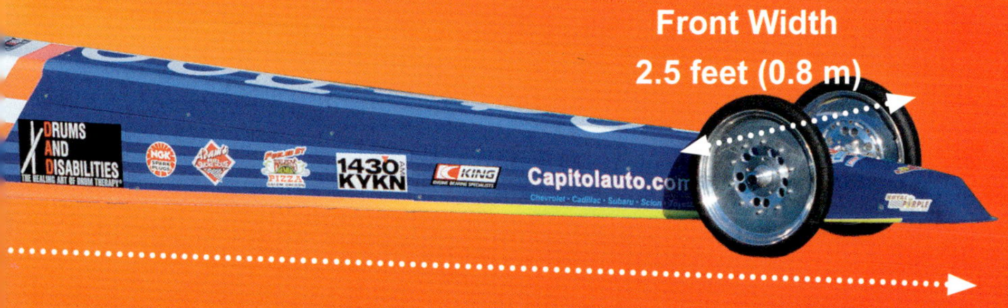

# BEYOND THE BOOK

After reading the book, it's time to think about what you learned. Try the following exercises to jumpstart your ideas.

## THINK

**DIFFERENT SOURCES.** Think about the different types of sources you might be able to find on Top Fuel dragsters. How would each kind of source be useful in its own way?

## CREATE

**SHARPEN YOUR RESEARCH SKILLS.** Safety is really important for drag racing. Where could you go in the library, or who could you talk to, to find more information about racing safety? Create a research plan by writing a paragraph detailing your next steps for research.

## SHARE

**SUM IT UP.** Write one paragraph summarizing the important points from the whole book. Make sure to write in your own words, rather than just copying what is in the text. Then, share the paragraph with a classmate. Does your classmate have any feedback on the summary or additional questions about dragsters?

## GROW

**REAL-LIFE RESEARCH.** What kinds of real-world places could you visit to do more research on dragsters? What other topics could you explore at this place?

# RESEARCH NINJA

Visit www.ninjaresearcher.com/0547 to learn how to take your research skills and book report writing to the next level!

## RESEARCH

**DIGITAL LITERACY TOOLS**

### SEARCH LIKE A PRO
Learn about how to use search engines to find useful websites.

### FACT OR FAKE?
Discover how you can tell a trusted website from an untrustworthy resource.

### TEXT DETECTIVE
Explore how to zero in on the information you need most.

### SHOW YOUR WORK
Research responsibly—learn how to cite sources.

## WRITE

### GET TO THE POINT
Learn how to express your main ideas.

### PLAN OF ATTACK
Learn prewriting exercises and create an outline.

**DOWNLOADABLE REPORT FORMS**

# Further Resources

## BOOKS

Bell, Samantha S. *Building Race Cars*. Focus Readers, 2018.

Lanier, Wendy Hinote. *Dragsters*. Focus Readers, 2017.

Monnig, Alex. *Behind the Wheel of a Dragster*. Child's World, 2016.

## WEBSITES

**FACTSURFER**

Factsurfer.com gives you a safe, fun way to find more information.

1. Go to www.factsurfer.com.
2. Enter "Dragsters" into the search box and click 🔍.
3. Select your book cover to see a list of related websites.

# Glossary

**accelerate:** To accelerate means to go faster. Racers want to see how quickly their car can accelerate.

**adrenaline:** Adrenaline is a chemical that is released in the brain during times of stress or excitement. The danger of drag racing sends a rush of adrenaline to the driver's brain.

**burnout:** Someone does a burnout by spinning a car's wheels very quickly without moving the vehicle. Drag racers do burnouts before each race so the tires can get a better grip on the track.

**chassis:** A chassis is the frame that supports a vehicle. A dragster's chassis has to be sturdy, but it must also be flexible enough so it doesn't crack.

**drag:** Drag is the reverse force that slows a car down. Parachutes created drag so the Funny Car could stop safely.

**hot rods:** Hot rods are regular cars that have been changed to be bigger, faster, or more powerful. At the Bonneville Salt Flats, racers competed in their hot rods.

**modified:** When something is modified, it is changed from its original design. Dragsters have modified chassis.

**nitromethane:** Nitromethane is a very flammable liquid that generates a lot of power when used as fuel in vehicles like Top Fuel dragsters. The driver carefully poured nitromethane into her fuel tank.

**spark plugs:** Spark plugs give off a spark of electricity that ignites the fuel in a car's engine. Dragsters give off so much heat that their spark plugs melt.

# Index



## PHOTO CREDITS

The images in this book are reproduced through the courtesy of: Orientaly/Shutterstock Images, front cover (background); Phillip Rubino/Shutterstock Images, front cover (car); Steve Mann/Shutterstock Images, pp. 3, 16–17; Philip Pilosian/Shutterstock Images, pp. 4–5, 29; Michael Stokes/Shutterstock Images, pp. 6–7; Avigator Fortuner/Shutterstock Images, p. 8; Action Sports Photography/Shutterstock Images, pp. 8–9, 15 (center), 18–19, 22–23, 30; Galyna Andrushko/Shutterstock Images, pp. 10–11; Christopher Halloran/Shutterstock Images, pp. 11, 15 (top); Joshua Rainey Photography/Shutterstock Images, pp. 12, 26–27 (bottom); David Allio/Icon Sportswire/AP Images, p. 15 (bottom); Boykov/Shutterstock Images, p. 20 (top); dan_prat/iStockphoto, p. 20 (bottom); Mark Long/AP Images, p. 21; Jkuecker/Shutterstock Images, pp. 24–25; Hohlovmihail/Shutterstock Images, p. 27 (top).

## ABOUT THE AUTHOR

Martha London lives in the Twin Cities. She writes children's books full-time. When she isn't writing, you can find her hiking in the woods.

# READING CORNER


Kelley, K. C. *Baby Bears*. North Mankato, Minn.: Amicus, 2018.

Niver, Heather Moore. *How Bears Grow Up*. New York: Enslow, 2017.

Schuetz, Kari. *Baby Bears*. Minneapolis: Bellwether Media, 2014.

# INDEX